Typology of career paths of int
Top Women Manager

£17.00

Bettina Al-Sadik-Lowinski

Typology of career paths of international Top Women Managers -
Global orientation pattern for qualified women in management

Typologie der Karrierewege von internationalen Topmanagerinnen -
Orientierungsmuster für qualifizierte Frauen im Management

Bibliografische Information der Deutschen Nationalbibliothek
Die Deutsche Nationalbibliothek verzeichnet diese Publikation in der
Deutschen Nationalbibliografie; detaillierte bibliographische Daten sind im Internet
über http://dnb.d-nb.de abrufbar.
1. Aufl. - Göttingen: Cuvillier, 2021

© CUVILLIER VERLAG, Göttingen 2021
  Nonnenstieg 8, 37075 Göttingen
  Telefon: 0551-54724-0
  Telefax: 0551-54724-21
  www.cuvillier.de

Alle Rechte vorbehalten. Ohne ausdrückliche Genehmigung des Verlages ist
es nicht gestattet, das Buch oder Teile daraus auf fotomechanischem Weg
(Fotokopie, Mikrokopie) zu vervielfältigen.
1. Auflage, 2021
Gedruckt auf umweltfreundlichem, säurefreiem Papier aus nachhaltiger Forstwirtschaft.
  ISBN 978-3-7369-7431-9
  eISBN 978-3-7369-6431-0

Dr. Bettina Al-Sadik-Lowinski, MCC,
Researcher, Author & Speaker
Founder of the Global Women Career Lab

www.globalwomencareerlab.com

edited by: Ian Lawrance, Australia

Content:

1. Typology of career paths of international Top Women Managers
2. Summary in German language
3. Bibliography

1. Typology of career paths of international Top Women Managers – Global orientation pattern for qualified women in management

> Women worldwide are still often the minority in top management so the career paths and patterns of successful role models can offer guidance and real inspiration for other women. Career typologies of women in senior management functions can support other women when they set their career plans and need to make decisions.
>
> One outcome of the international research driven from the Global Women Career Lab is an intercultural career typology of top women managers in various countries, which offers valuable insights into women strategies for building careers. The typology analysis role model focuses on how women who achieved top management positions around the world built their careers and the characteristics go with it. The analysis describes the five career types which were most frequent in the research group.
>
> Different to the handful of existing typologies for women in management, the majority of the women researched here show patterns and paths where career decisions are not made with a focus on family or other external conditions. Most women have pursued an unbounded career, often globally and changing employers in order to rise up the corporate hierarchy.
>
> Experienced coaches can use the Global Women Career Lab typology to stimulate reflection on career decisions and shed light on the choices of women in management levels. The typology also shows HR experts that talented women chose companies according to the opportunities they offered for women to rise in senior management.

According to a global study by Grant Thornton, the average proportion of women in senior management positions worldwide was twenty nine percent in 2020 and has risen slowly since 2014. Women remain under-represented at the top of the corporate hierarchy in most countries around the world. In many places, „pioneering female CEOs" continue to be celebrated and this only highlights the growing stagnation. Even though women worldwide are still a minority in upper management positions the situation differs on the world map. Countries like Russia, China and France have a higher proportion of women in senior management whereas Germany or Japan are on the lower ranks (Thornton 2017,2018,2019).

Having more women in management positions delivers greater benefits for companies and more economic power for countries. Although the proportion of women in middle management positions has increased worldwide, equality between men and women in senior management has yet to be achieved. A Peterson Institute for International Economics survey of 21,980 listed companies in 91 countries found that a higher proportion of female managers in a company equates to higher profitability. Research by McKinsey and Women Matter (2012), Catalyst (2016) and Noland at the Petersen Institute (2016) shows that a higher proportion of women on company boards delivers higher profits and better overall company performance. These findings are confirmed by other research around the world. A variety of studies and views exist as to the causes, however, the continued dearth of female role models is well-recognized and the number of women in senior corporate positions is still low.

In order to increase the presence of women in C-suite functions various actions have been put into place in different countries on political, societal and organizational levels. Furthermore, the support of qualified women, for example, through tailored coaching for women leaders, can be an effective tool to support women rising on an individual level. Areas like career planning and the right decision making with career alternatives have an important function in coaching women leaders.

The research of the Global Women Career Lab (Al-Sadik-Lowinski 2017, 2018, 2020) offers a wealth of knowledge about female careers and leadership in various cultural contexts. It also provides tools such as the FemCareer-Model and the FemCareer-Assessment for coaching women leaders to rise to their next career level. One result of the ongoing international research is an intercultural career typology of top women managers in various countries such as France, China, Japan, Russia and Germany. Typologies solely focused on women in top management are still rare in literature despite offering valuable insights into women strategies with career building. Career typologies can support women in their career planning and decisions as they offer role model patterns for how women who achieved top management positions around the world built their careers and what characteristics go with it.

Qualified women benefit from more intercultural research into the careers of top female managers

Looking at the available research on women in senior management, it is striking that career research in the field of management has for a long time focused exclusively on the experiences of men. One reason for this is surely the fact that the numbers of women in top management worldwide have historically been limited and were based on a male perspective. More and more international researchers, such as O'Neil (2013) and Lepine (1992), are developing women-specific approaches because they believe that women's careers follow different patterns than those of men. Even if conventional, hierarchically structured careers still predominate in many companies around the world today, career patterns other than the purely traditional ones can already be observed amongst women. This is reflected in the career paths of the high-flying women surveyed in the Global Women Career Lab research. International research on women in top management positions is rare, compared to in-country studies. While several researchers have analyzed the careers of women within countries, multinational observations are rare, partly due to the complexities of data collection.

Women career typologies offer valuable information for coaching women leaders

One result of the ongoing international research is an intercultural career typology of top women managers in various countries. Career typologies can support women in their career planning and decisions. They offer role model patterns showing how women who already achieved top management positions around the world have built their careers and what characteristics go with it. Women in executive management have a number of questions to answer during their career paths. Questions about changing companies or not and if they are changing, based on what criteria, moving abroad or staying local, and questions about pursuing specialist paths versus broader paths are some of the important decisions which women are facing. These are supplemented by questions connected with the typical determinants of women careers such as gender equality, family organization, women's career orientation and motivation. Each career type combines various determinants which have been identified of being important for the success of women leaders in management. This research-based typology can be used during coaching of women in management functions around the globe to stimulate career decisions and consideration of choices.

The Global Women Career Lab: Research-based analysis of the career paths of female role models in leading economies

The Global Women Career Lab is a unique international research project carried out in five countries from 2014 until 2020. A total of 110 women in top executive positions at multinational companies participated. To date, women in senior management positions from economically leading nations - France, Germany, Russia, Japan and China - participated. The economies considered in this research represent the upper, middle and lower portions of the global rankings for the number of women in managerial positions.

The career paths of these women involved more than 500 companies worldwide, with work being undertaken in over 21 countries. For the research-based, empirical study the top female executives, qualitative in-depth interviews were carried out.

All of the women interviewed here are executives in leading positions, primarily working in international companies. The women were selected through a process based on theoretical sampling. Semi-structured, problem-centered interviews were conducted to collect empirical data, which was evaluated and analyzed using a scientific approach, with the help of reductive qualitative structured content analysis. Parts of this project formed a dissertation overseen by the University of Burgundy in France.

So how are women's career paths and pattern currently handled? They are being compromised by longstanding tension between society's view of what roles women should play, the opportunities for women in companies and the goals and constraints of the women themselves. A variety of contextual factors influence the progression of a female manager's career. The analysis in the Global Women Career Lab is based on a framework called the FemCareer-Model (Al-Sadik-Lowinski, 2017) in which important determinants of women's careers are encapsulated. The model was the guiding principle for the interviews with 110 top female executives as well as for the evaluation; it helped serve as the road map for the overall research, analysis and typology.

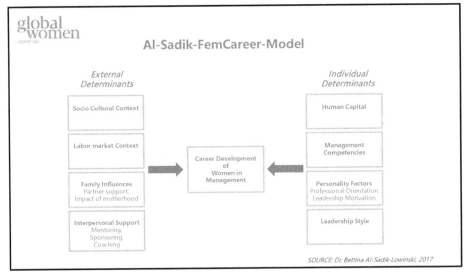

Figure 1: **The FemCareer-Model** (Al-Sadik-Lowinski, 2017)

The Female Career Model focuses on external determinants and individual influences on the careers of female senior executives that result in different career paths and plans. These paths and patterns are regarded as being tangibly affected – to a greater or lesser extent – by determinants. The paths and pattern have both descriptive and evaluative components.

The external influences are ones that impact on women's careers from the outside in the form of overarching conditions. External influences derive from the cultural traditions of society, the labor market situation, specific aspects of gender policy, familial situations and interpersonal support. Interpersonal support refers to personal support systems such as networks, mentors and supportive superiors. Taken together, these factors form the external framework within which the women's careers develop.

Individual influences are made up of aspects that are specific to the participants, grounded in their personal backgrounds and personalities, and linked to their career paths. They include their educational backgrounds, particular skills, aspects of their personalities that are relevant to their careers and their specific leadership styles. Career paths are associated with individual assessments of career success and can be expressed through various factors such as individuals' personal level of satisfaction and the position they have achieved in an organization's hierarchy. Paths describe the particular positions a person has held over the course of their career and the choices they have made. The model is also informed by findings from current literature on women's careers and incorporates critical career determinants which are not limited to particular countries.

The total number of interviewed women, 110, is big for a qualitative research project but does not allow for generalizations to be made and must be interpreted in the context of a qualitative research. Quasi-statistical analysis, however, was carried out in subcategories where it made sense to do so and provides a picture of the women´s preferred career types and pattern.

The results by country have been careful interpreted in the cultural and economic context of each country. Interested readers can learn more about the specific socio cultural and economic gender situation of each country in the more detailed, overall publication of the research (Al-Sadik-Lowinski, 2020).

Participants of the Global Women Career Lab research - a carefully selected sample with role modeling character

The participants in the Global Women Career Lab come from China, Russia, Japan, Germany and France and represent a wide age range. The 110 women selected for the Global Women Career Lab were between 32 and 63 years old. The majority were 45-55 years old. The women over 60 came from China, Germany and France. The companies in which the women worked at the time of the interviews are primarily global businesses, only some local companies where included. The career paths of the women selected cover more than 500 companies across the globe. It was important that the women chosen to take part in the research represented a broad range of sectors. Overall, the women worked in over 20 different sectors, with a focus on Industry and Service. The Industry sector, for example, covered many different areas of business including automotive, pharmaceuticals, steel processing, household, food, consulting, fashion, travel, luxury goods, telecommunications, media and more.

Theoretical sampling was used to ensure that the appropriate women were selected in keeping with the research questions to be covered. The sampling for the lab was driven by a separate definition of "women in top management" which included hierarchical positions of the level one (CEO, GM) and minus one. In addition, the following areas were important for the selection of women: their freedom of decision making, the degree of influence on corporate strategy, personal responsibility, budget responsibility and the number of employees. Only salaried women, not women entrepreneurs, were considered for the research investigation.

Background from management literature: Women's career patterns exhibit a wider range and variety than those of men

The career patterns developed with a view to women's careers in existing research are of significance to the analysis of the finding of the Global Women Career Lab. Career patterns serve as a theoretical foundation and framework of reference. Several researchers have addressed questions concerning career patterns and paths (Lepine, 1992; Lyness and Thompson, 2000; O'Neil et al., 2008) in order to describe women's career patterns more precisely. A career path is generally defined as a trajectory of work-related experiences in which an individual has engaged over the course of their life. It describes how a person progresses from their first job to their current one. A career pattern can be defined as a consistent and recurring characteristic or trait that helps to characterise a career and serves as an indicator or model for predicting future career behaviour. These two concepts are often used interchangeably in the literature. Vinkenburg and Weber (2012) analysed managerial career patterns in a review of empirical studies. They state that the existing empirical evidence on managerial career patterns is rather limited and that upward mobility is still the norm, even when contrasted with "new" careers. Familiar, traditional paths are typified by strong upwards mobility and leave little space for sideways moves or frequent changes of organisation. These paths demand advancement-oriented executives who strive for a vertical career. Lehnert (1996) describes "serpentine" careers, where employees rise up the ranks by switching between organisations. This career form still follows a fixed path that remains relatively similar to the traditional career path. However, the possibility of changing job requirements is integral to this career type.

Several researchers suggest that women's careers are uniquely different from men's and exhibit a broader range and variety of paths (Hurley and Sonnenfeld, 1997; Lepine, 1992; O'Neil et al., 2008). Patterns range from traditional, hierarchical advancement and corporate ladders (Lyness and Thompson, 2000), to "snake-like" patterns (Richardson, 1996) and "zigzag patterns" (Gersick and Kram, 2002). Research participants of Gersick and Kram described their career paths as zigzag-like. The findings suggest that women experience transitional periods pegged to the turn of each decade of their lives, involving shifts in the content and priority of one or more elements of their life structure. These periods are reflected in their career development and differ in various ways from those of men. Half of the women in Lepines (1992) research are employed in a traditional upwardly mobile career and the other half in patterns that can be categorised as downward, lateral, transitory or static. A somewhat divergent but fundamentally similar account is offered by Huang and Sverke (2007), who describe women's occupational paths as diverse, exhibiting patterns such as upward mobility, stability, downward mobility and fluctuation. Hurley and Sonnenfeld (1997), meanwhile, investigated the question of whether the tournament model of career as a series of wins and losses in a race to the top is applicable to women's careers. They concluded that the model is not valid for women to the same degree. All these approaches address the distinctive features of women's careers and attempt to express these features in models that replace or expand traditional patterns. These models are associated with dynamism, mobility, flexibility and employability to a greater or lesser extent

O'Neil et al. (2004) combined sociological factors, path and context, and psychological factors, choice and control, in their career model. Patterns were characterised as a continuum between ordered (planned, organised) and emergent (serendipitous, circuitous). The ordered pattern can be characterised as being strategically planned and executed. An emergent career follows a reactive rather than a proactive path, with unexpected twists and turns and serendipitous events. It is designed to accommodate aspects of one's life other than traditional work. The "kaleidoscope career" exhibits aspects of an emergent career. Loci were characterised on a continuum between external and internal. An internal locus is manifested in the belief that one is responsible for one's own career and is in charge of creating and managing one's career by oneself. An external locus expresses the belief that the course that a career takes is caused by chance or other external interventions, such as networks or contacts from which career opportunities emanate. The career patterns developed with a view to women's careers that have been described above are of significance when analysing the findings of the Global Women Career Lab. They form a theoretical foundation and framework of reference.

The Career typology of top women managers around the globe

The first criterion for developing the typology driving the research of the Global Women Career Lab was the women's career paths. The first step was to assess whether the career path was "bounded" (organizational career constrained to a single company) and followed a traditional linear or ladder-like structure, or if the career path was "boundaryless" (as per DeFillippi and Arthur, 1994) with no ties or only weak ties to particular companies. Boundaryless careers were defined as "sequences of job opportunities that go beyond the boundaries of a single employment setting". Traditional bounded or "organizational careers", on the other hand, evolve within the context of a single company (Arthur and Rousseau, 2001).

In accordance with the definitions of O'Neil et al. (2004) it was also assessed whether careers were ordered or emergent. Alongside these criteria, the typology also incorporated geographic mobility as this was of great importance in most of the career paths included in this study. Distinctions are drawn between international mobility, local mobility within one country and career paths confined to one metropole. The career determinants that had a particular impact on different subgroups were taken from among the external and individual factors described in the original research publication (Al-Sadik-Lowinski, 2017). It was assessed which factors had a stronger or weaker impact on the women's career paths. The women's personalities and motivations were criteria that could be derived from the individual determinants. The classification of impact as strong or weak was based on the women's descriptions and, in line with the qualitative character of the study as a whole; the classification is not quantified on a scale. The classification is hence subjective and unsuitable for quantitative comparisons.

Table 1 shows an overview of the five career patterns that emerged from the analysis of the career paths. How strongly the determinants influenced the careers was defined as follows: "(Very) High" refers to factors that are highly and continuously relevant for the career paths of all the women in a particular subgroup. "Medium" refers to career determinants that were described a few times by some of the women in this group. "Low" refers to factors that were described as being of little or no relevance, were not mentioned at all or were mentioned by less than ten percent of the women in the group. The results are presented in percentage, as the country group sizes differ slightly with the Chinese mainland group being the biggest sample and the Japanese group being the smallest. The descriptions incorporate the earlier findings from the qualitative content analysis of the group as a whole. The main characteristics of the different types are described in detail below.

The top women managers feel responsible for their own career advancement and in charge of managing it

The results of the analysis suggest there is a more internal career locus by the great majority of the women, defined as the belief that one is responsible for one's own career and in charge of managing it. Few responses in the group pointed to a more external career locus, whereby a career occurs as a result of chance or other external interventions from which the career opportunities emanate. When the accounts are analysed as a whole, however, such responses are always subordinate to the women's own goal-focused career planning and desire for career advancement.

Another factor that became apparent in the women's descriptions of their planned career steps was how self-reliant they are in planning their careers. Although they attribute a role to factors such as chance and opportunity or being in the right place at the right time for determining the paths their careers have taken, what predominates in the women's descriptions is their own proactive action, initiative and planning: spotting opportunities and then seizing them. These descriptions suggest an internal career locus.

For these women, career planning relates to exposure and looking for allies. The women specifically looked for and accepted positions that promised a high level of exposure in their companies. According to the women, exposure increases their chances of advancing further. Here once again, the women took the initiative and planned how they could maximise their visibility in their companies. They also involved key decision-makers in their career plans and continuously worked to win and retain their support. What is relevant here is the women's individual planning and the ways in which they exerted influence on these connections. These factors also support the attribution of an internal career locus in keeping with the definition by O'Neil.

Five patterns of women in senior management: Bounded – Unbounded global – Stop and Go – Flexible hoppers – Lean on and move up

The five career types which have been analysed in this global research can stand as exemplary for typical career pattern of successful women who rose to very senior positions over the course of their careers. Women at early stages could use these types to discuss with their mentor or coach which pattern appeals to them more and which one less. In later career stages, women can use the typology to reflect on their choices. Is the chosen path still the right one for their overall direction in life, or is change a better alternative? The typology allows women in management to identify areas which need to be clarified and the best fit pattern for their professional circumstances and their individual life goals. In executive coaching the typology can be a resonant framework to reflect and foster individual choices.

The chart below provides a breakdown of the career types of top women managers interviewed.

Chart 1: Global Career Typology of top women managers- breakdown of five career types of women in senior management

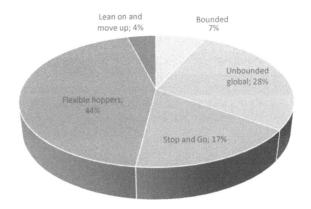

The main characteristics of the different types are described in detail below, followed by an overall conclusion.

Table 1: Global Career Pattern Typology of top women managers
(Al-Sadik-Lowinski, 2021)

	Bounded	Unbounded Global	Stop and go	Flexible hoppers	Lean on and move up
Career path	Bounded	Unbounded			
Mobility	Local/global	Global	Local/global	Local	Local
Pattern	Ordered ladder	Ordered linear	Emergent	Ordered serpentine	Emergent/ ordered
Career locus	Internal	Internal	Internal	Internal	External
Determinant					
Individual Motivation	Organisational Loyalty	Achievement orientation Assertiveness	Balance roles	Assertiveness, curiosity and variety	Loyalty to mentor Developing others
Career orientation	very high	very high	high	very high	high
Family orientation	Low	Low	medium to high	Low	Medium
Mentoring/ Sponsoring	High	Medium	Low	Medium (various)	Very high
Networking internal	very high	high	medium	high	very high
Networking external	high	very high	medium	very high	medium
Chinese mainland	10%	29%	23%	29%	9%
Chinese overseas	no	23%	48%	29%	no
German	12%	47%	no	41%	no
French	12%	24%	12%	46%	6%
Russian	no	6%	12%	82%	no
Japanese	no	57%	no	43%	no
Total Research group	7%	28%	17%	44%	4%

15

1. Bounded

> *Women with traditional, hierarchical bounded paths, who pursue their whole career in only one company, are a minority in the Global Women Career Lab. Their paths do not reflect the typical HR requirements of today's senior management. Despite this, women in this group can, and do, still rise to the highest corporate levels.*

This career type only applies to 7% of all top women managers in the Global Women Career Lab, a distinct minority. These women's career paths are typified by a strong bond with their companies. This is typical of traditional, ladder-like career paths which according to career theory were common in the past and still remain so today in many cases, especially at large companies in countries such as Germany and France. All of the women in this group have only worked at a single company: there has been no intercompany mobility, and their careers can be described as bounded and upwards linear or ladder-like. This type was not found in the Russian and Japanese groups, which was surprising as in Japan bounded careers are usually the mainstream.

The bounded women have often reached highest levels within their company, being GM or CEO level, as well as chief supervisory board levels. They have responsibility for the whole company or major units at a national level. They have held a diverse range of positions in their companies, and hence have wide-ranging experience within the companies.

All women in this subtype of the global typology have internal career loci and plan their careers strategically with a focus on their company's corporate system and what it offers to them. All of the women associate career success with hierarchical advancement. Although there are other factors, the individual motivation of women in this group can be best described by organisational loyalty and adaptation to one corporate culture.

Over the course of their careers, the bounded women have demonstrated a high degree of flexibility and adaptability in responding to their company's requirements. This is evident in the women assuming responsibility for various areas. In doing so, they have developed their knowledge and experience strategically, which is characteristic of ordered career paths. These women got to know the corporate system of their company very well, understand the importance of alliances and used the power system of their specific employer strategically to rise to the highest company levels. All the women have a strong colleague network at their company's headquarters. External networks are also strong, but the focus of building alliances is internal for this group of women.

The careers of bounded women are evenly spread between national and global roles. Very national based careers are evident in some women in Europe, while most Chinese women were globally bounded. Older women typically have locally bounded careers whereas the younger women are more comfortable to change countries with the same company and later return to the head office.

In the group of Chinese women, it is notable that bounded careers pattern were typically showing with women working for German companies. These women were relocating between

Germany and China for the same German DAX companies. Choosing to study in Germany and to work for a German company in China were actively planned steps of these Chinese top leaders. The first phase of their careers took place in Germany, however, they were already firmly planning to return to China to pursue their professions with the same company during their career paths. Besides in Germany, there were no other cases of Chinese women with a bounded pattern working for other European companies.

All bounded women moved from staff jobs held at the outset of their careers to line jobs fairly rapidly, within four years. They looked actively for opportunities within their company and used the company system to broaden their leadership experiences and management competencies. They also change jobs in order to rise within the system or create their own jobs within the system.

M.C., Executive board member, France: The management at the time wanted to create a private bank. That hadn't existed until that point. The idea was to establish a special private banking operation using existing networks. Basically, this led to me taking on the creation of this new division. The establishment of a company with a small team, we were five or six people at the beginning, and we created this private banking business, which became the first private bank in France, which today generates €100 billion in assets. So, I was chosen for the job and I took it. And so we created a model which we then adapted to every country and culture and regulation, in Belgium, Italy, Luxembourg, Morocco, Poland, Turkey, the United States, in all the countries where the bank actually had a network. I spent about ten years on it. It was really fabulous. And then I was appointed director of the French network. This is a very important position in a bank, of course. That position put me on the board, and I was the first woman on it. And this position had previously always been held by men who were from ENA, polytechnics, they were always from the Grandes Écoles. Then I arrived, a woman with a high school diploma. So, it was very unusual. And so, I held this position for seven years, it was me without a doubt who held it the longest. I was chosen because I knew the entire company network really well, because I had the first part of my career in that network really, so I knew really well how it worked. I also knew the clients very well. On the other hand, I did not know much about the private banking profession. Of course, I also had standing. And I accepted this position, which was a risk. It is very important when you're on a particular path to be convinced that there will be opportunities that you can take and at the same time to be prepared to accept risks. And so that's how I did it. And it was great. It went extremely well. And once the French model had been developing well for a while, I exported it. So, I travelled with the team to 13 different countries. So, it was really a start-up that went international. And so, with the small team that I had, and without having any actual managerial authority, I went and visited all the private banks that we had created in those countries. It was all about the power of influence and conviction.

Being bounded with a local focus does not mean that women do not have the flexibility to travel frequently and far. Women in France of this type, lead global projects and frequently travel around the world as part of the job. One example from China spent four years in charge of a global project and about sixty percent of her time was travelling to other locations, such as Europe and India, while staying based in China. Only one top women manager from Germany has a very local-orientated path involving little travel, focused very strongly on - and targeting - her home culture rather than building up international expertise.

M., Supervisory board member, Head of Communications, Germany: Well, I've never really managed to leave Germany. Today, it's taken for granted in DAX companies, it's assumed that everyone'll complete at least two international assignments before they can progress to a management position. In other words, it is standard these days, everyone who wants a leadership position here has to get some international experience. Communication is a very German affair. I have to have a good command of German language, I have to be able to network and I have to have my contacts here on site. And, if you've done international projects, then it will always have been with agencies. Sure, they have to be managed, but then you have teams too. So, for me it wasn't a big deal to build on my skills in this area as far as I could. In any case, I would have had zero chance in marketing either here or anywhere else. I just don't have the profile you need for that these days, or that you would have needed even in the past, to work in marketing. I don't have the experience or any of the other things you need to have. It's a very niche area, definitely. And one which allows you to move up through the company with little or no international experience.

Family has not been a major influencing factor for this group. Half of the women have children and are married to husbands who are less ambitious about their careers. The other women are childless or single. The woman in this group with children exhibit a particularly high level of local geographic mobility, for example one of the Chinese women travels long distances between work in Beijing and family in Shanghai. Otherwise, the women in the bounded group are frequently on business trips overseas like, for example, the French women.

2. Unbounded global

> *Unbounded global women show intercompany and intercountry mobility even if they are mothers. Flexibility and assertiveness are characteristics of these highly strategical top women managers*

The second largest subgroup of the analysis covers 28% of the top women managers globally surveyed are the unbounded global. Women who were assigned to the unbounded global group have spent time abroad in several countries on one or more occasions. Most of them studied abroad, and all have worked abroad on one or more occasions. These women's career paths are typified by a flexible choice of companies, especially at the start of their careers. This flexibility extends to the nationality of the companies' head office, inter-firm mobility and place of work. Their careers can be described as boundaryless and upwards linear. The women's intercompany mobility mostly tended to decrease later in their careers as they attained senior roles.

The women in this group have reached the full range of senior levels classed as selection criteria for this study. Some highest-ranking women, with the title of president, are in this group, as well as CFOs, VP level and senior directors. Some have experience in a broad range of different departments, others have worked exclusively in finance or sales.

The unbounded top women managers have internal career loci, with highly strategic global career planning. They place emphasis on actively reflecting on their personal career ambitions and goals. These women are very flexible, both in terms of geographic mobility and accepting new responsibilities, and use challenges as an opportunity for advancement. They have strategically planned their own careers. Changes of location do not represent barriers, rather, they are firmly integrated into their plans and goals. All the women associate career success with hierarchical advancement. The women in this group are typified by very high achievement orientation coupled with strong assertiveness.

B., CMO, German: When I was with the company back home, I was in international marketing, of course. That's such a great job. I mean, there's no better job than marketing, let's say, beauty products. And flying all over the world and doing photo shoots. But then, of course, at some point you say to yourself, hold on, it can't go on like this. The discrimination against women was pretty high. And then at some point I said to myself, "I need to think about this whole thing a bit more clearly, how I want things to be from now on." And that's when I started thinking much more strategically. What positions, what moves, what do I need to do. Well, the first time, I definitely wanted to be a managing director. That was a very clear goal. And then I did career planning again once I was a managing director, which I actually was three times. In three different companies. You learn that you can actually do considerably more than you thought you could. For me, that was decisive. I was in Spain during the crisis. And we were actually being very successful there. And from then on, I actually thought, well, maybe I could actually aim a lot higher. At next company in France, when we were having problems with the German business. That was actually how I negotiated the thing with my boss. When I was head of marketing for Europe, I said to him: "We're having problems in Germany. You have nobody to solve it for you. If you send me, I'll solve it. And in return, you make me managing director." That's the deal we made. I was there for six months again later on. So, it's important to plan your career. You need to have a planning horizon too. You must really think about where you want to be at the end of it. And go for particular positions in a fairly targeted manner. I've just become a board member in the US for an

American company. That was one of the goals I set for myself. I talked to people about it for about a year. So, I know a lot of people who knew I'd like to do it.

L., GM, French: I don't know, but I know it was a very deliberate decision, so I studied maths and physics in high school and then studied finance because, for me, the fact that it might be more male dominated jobs, didn't mean I couldn't do it and I think I wanted to show that I could do it. It was actually easier for me than literature or marketing. I really wanted to go to Harvard, and in fact I applied, almost only to Harvard because I really wanted to go there. I wanted to have an experience in the United States. Study in the USA, work in the USA, really discover the world. I funded it and borrowed a lot of money to get to Harvard. I think it was a childhood dream. It was planned to some extent, although it is a bit of luck. After that I worked for a famous US company because I could learn management there. Then it was important that I wanted to enter the consumer sector, from the Technology and Finance to a French luxury company. I mean, they would never have hired me, never because luxury goods, it's an industry where we want people who have that luxury background. If they had, they would have hired me for a job that wasn't interesting. I think that is why I got into the US consulting firm because I saw it as a learning experience, and it was possible from there.

The unbounded global career pattern was evident as the strongest in the German and Japanese research group. The women work in different industries and at different companies in a variety of number of regions including the US, Europe and Asia, as well as Australia and South Africa. German women have worked in countries such as the US, Asia and other European countries and had one to four assignments outside their home country. French women have worked in the US, Canada, the French speaking European countries; three of them have worked in Asia. The Chinese women have worked in average in two to four different countries outside China. The Japanese women have worked in the US and only one single case in Sweden. In the overall unbounded global group, the number of companies the women have worked at ranges from three to eight.

M., Head of Supply Chain, Japanese: When I worked in Silicon Valley, in a U.S. based company, I really learnt the need to self-promote myself and sell myself, because that's not what I was taught when I was growing up. In Japan, it seemed more virtuous to be accepted by society, you want to be – especially women, you are not really taught or encouraged to sell yourself. Also negotiate, one thing I learnt in my business school and also in my job in the U.S., I learned how to negotiate, I learnt how to say no, so all these things, probably, I have more than the typical Japanese woman. My husband and I we were supposed to be split between Minnesota and Cincinnati. I was telling my sponsor, "I'll be based out of Cincinnati, my husband will be based out of Minnesota, and we'll just meet each other on the weekends." My sponsor said, "Why would you do that? There are similar opportunities for your husband to work here in Cincinnati." He went off to find a research lab that had what my husband could possibly work at through his connections. He was able to establish that connection through so that my husband was able to work in Cincinnati. I think he went far beyond what a normal sponsor would do. [laughs] I had mentors for different things and including becoming another type of mentor or having even a male mentor, female mentors, other organization mentors and I think I was lucky to have different mentors throughout my journey.

Some of the women in the unbounded global group described how they were supported by mentors they chose themselves. However, this factor is only a moderately strong determinant of this group's career development. The top women managers have a focus on very strong external global networks, although internal networking and company alliances are also important to them.

Family has not been a major influencing factor for this group. Several of these women described how they prioritised their careers over the demands of family roles. The women from China had family situations that differed from most in the overall China group. More Chinese women in the unbounded group are childless and single. Several of these women with family described how they prioritised their careers over the demands of familial roles. For instance, one interviewee lived away from her child on other continents for several years. Another woman left behind a potential life partner in the UK to take up a position in China. The French, German and Japanese women did not differ from the rest of their national research group in this respect. There was no connection between being single or childless with regards to being an unbounded global career type.

3. Stop and Go

> *Women tend to make holistic career choices that consider family demands and relationships. In this research on top women managers, the Stop and Go sub-group counts for only 16 % of all women. The women come from countries with high participation of women in top management. A hypothesis from the results is that in countries with low participation in top management, this career type would not reach senior levels.*

This sub-group of the Global Women Career Lab seems to be comparable to the few other published typologies with women from western countries in which over forty percent of the women make career changes due to family demands or follow their husbands to a different city or country (Lepine 1992). These women made holistic choices that take relationships, constraints and opportunities into consideration. In this global research only 17 % of the overall group were assigned to this subgroup. This includes women from China and Russia. The women in this group also shift the patterns of their careers by rotating different aspects of their lives so as to arrange their relationships and roles in new ways. Their career paths can be categorised as boundaryless as these women also move between companies and sometimes countries in order to rise to higher levels. All but one of the women in this group have children, on average two.

Surprisingly, the group contains no women from Germany or Japan, where motherhood is one of the strongest determinants for women careers. One possible interpretation for this could be that, in environments where top female managers are still an exception, this career type would not lead to a senior management function.
The highest percentage found is amongst Chinese women working overseas. Most of them are married to a German or French man and will stay long term in Europe. The expat Chinese women who return to China do not usually belong to this sub-group. The Chinese women with European husbands are balancing their original strong career orientation which was developed in China with expectations to the mother role in their new European environment.

These women's career loci can be described as internal, since – despite a focus on their personal roles within their families at certain times – they manage their careers autonomously and creatively, continuously building up their expertise. Nonetheless, when asked whether they think they could have progressed further in their careers if, say, they had not had children, the women were relatively unanimous that they have accepted compromises in their career progression.

The frequency of company changes in this group is highly varied. Some women have changed companies twice, most have changed four times and one has worked in ten different companies. Again, these women cover the full spectrum of senior management roles. At the time of the interviews, they were GMs, VPs or senior directors. Some of the women were pursuing careers in HR. Other careers were centred on marketing, communications, finance and legal affairs. Their career paths are characterised by an alternation of upward and lateral moves with varying frequency. Many of the women have had career breaks when they went part-time, took time off or temporarily ran their own businesses. Some of them were even temporarily downgraded to more junior roles. However, the overall trajectory of all their careers is in the direction of continued hierarchical advancement. The main career determinants for these women are family and relationships. Their career paths are strongly emergent and involve responsiveness, fluid movement in and out of organisations and accommodation of non-work-related priorities.

The women in this group on average have two children; more than fifty percent have career-oriented husbands. In the overall research group women tend to have non-career-oriented husband. In particular, Chinese women with two or more children find themselves constantly trying to balance two different roles, career woman and mother. They receive emotional support from their husbands but little in the way of practical help that alleviates some of the demands placed on them. However, all the women also have housekeepers. It is notable that these women do not want to delegate certain aspects of their children's upbringing, such as helping their children with their homework. When asked if they have considered delegating some of these tasks, all have rejected the possibility. They see it as one of their core duties to help their children with their homework themselves.

H., VP China, with foreign husband: That's an interesting question. I think the decision to go part time after I had the second child, he pushed me definitely. I think if not for him, I don't know if I would come to the decision so quickly. I think I always had some thoughts about it, but he was understandable very concerned that my workload was very heavy. But I think we got a line on this very quickly. I don't think he pushed me into something I didn't want. But I think he probably pushed me to make the decision faster.

M., Director, Chinese in Germany: I think being married to a German has had a big impact on my thinking. He comes from a different environment and always thought differently than I did. So, I always learned, thought, learned, thought. The decision to come to Germany was not my husband's decision. This is because I know that my husband is different from me. He comes from this background, so I wanted to delve deeper into this culture. I think my mother-in-law has shaped my thinking a lot. She is a housewife, she raised 4 children, she is very happy and charming. I came to the conclusion from her that it is also nice to be a housewife for a certain time. In the end, she is happy and charming and makes a contribution to society as a whole. It's a good life.

Over the course of their careers, the women in this group have at times made decisions that prioritised family over career. Examples include going part-time after the birth of their second child, something that is unusual in China, or a woman who quit her job for the sake of her son and his school when her company relocated. In Russia, one interviewee took a break of two years which she than found long and difficult. One woman switched to another company because her husband was also pursuing his career at the company where she had originally worked. Another returned home from abroad after a relatively short time, even though she knew this would prevent further career progression, because her husband could not adapt to life in France. Three of the Chinese women gave up their jobs in China and followed their husbands abroad when the latter took up overseas positions for the sake of their own careers. Their career progression differed from conventional corporate career paths; for example, they did an MBA during a career break, started their own business or took up a post at a consultancy instead of continuing in a senior role in the previous company. In each of these cases, it was not possible for the women to seamlessly continue their careers in the other country, and so they adjusted their plans accordingly.

None of the women remained unemployed for long. Due to unconventional career steps that led them outside the corporate world, the women have accumulated a greater breadth of experience than the women in the other subgroups. Examples of the women's forays into independence and new experiences outside the corporate world included running an online service for export, providing consulting services for American companies who wanted to set up subsidiaries in China and running an internal university for a big-name American food company as a freelancer working from a remote home office. Some of the women in the group took short-term career breaks to have children or used the birth of a child as a pretext to take a break and change companies. There are also women who followed their partners abroad. However, none of the women relocated within their home country for the sake of their partners' careers. Women did not have less inter-firm mobility if they took a break when they gave birth or relocated abroad because of their partner.

4. Flexible hoppers

> In the Global Women Career Lab, a local career with high inter-firm mobility and low bonds to a specific company is the preferred career path of the top women managers. Women who are flexible hoppers go to where the chances for advancement are waiting. They have a high achievement motivation and possess the capability to adapt to different company cultures.

Women who pursued their careers exclusively in their home countries without spending time abroad were categorised in this group. With 44 %, it represents the highest number group of women in the global research survey. Russian and French women are strongly tied to this career type. In the other countries, this subtype is also strongly represented. The flexible hopper women have worked in four to nine different companies and exhibit an inter-firm mobility typical of a boundaryless career path. It is characteristic of these women's career paths that they deliberately choose hierarchical advancement without being bound to any particular company long-term. They go wherever the next career opportunity presents, and where the next higher position waits. They look for opportunities for advancement. Hence, their career paths can be categorised as boundaryless and can be described as rising by switching between employers. The women have reached GM, VP and national director levels. This group's geographic mobility is confined to mobility within their country, and in most cases confined to business centres such as Paris, Moscow and Shanghai. German women in this group show country-wide mobility between the major local business centres.

The main determinants of these women's careers are individual personality factors. They all have strong achievement orientation. All are highly assertive and curious, crave challenges and variety in their careers and want to learn a lot, as quickly as possible. These factors are also present in the overall group but based on the women's feedback, are especially pronounced among the flexible hoppers. They are also exceptionally focused on objective career success in the form of hierarchical advancement. The flexible hoppers have internal career loci; they plan and act in accordance with their individual career goals. They are also interested in continuous further development and incorporate this into their decisions and plans. The women possess high intercultural competence, in the sense of adapting to different company cultures. Their curiosity and strong desire to learn were driving factors that led to their exceptional capacity to identify, understand and adapt to cultural differences in management styles.

Russian Director: I tried to find a job by specialty, by my diploma, electronic engineer. Near my house, near my home, there is some electronic factory. It's sort of style, a former Soviet Union. Mostly they work for military and now became private, but it's producing some electronics. They opened a new department also with the government's budgeting. I wanted to design some part of Russian Satellite system. I am kind of open-minded and I could talk to American specialists, because this technology is not available in Russia, so we work with Germans, with Slovenians, with Americans. I even had some project and I became a business deputy of department. Later, I was disappointed because they didn't create, didn't design. It's a former Soviet Union factory, it felt old people like, around sixty years old. It's still the same mentality. The young generation mentality was different. I switched back to a tech company. They needed someone with my background who could communicate with Germans. Then I found a position at another company. It took me a year to do that. And then the crisis came and I worked for a Chinese company. Now I'm back in an American company. I always found the positions with my CV or now via LinkedIn.

A few women in this group also described unforeseen negative effects, insecurity and risks that can come with changing companies. These women described how changing companies did not lead to the next career step that they had hoped for. Changing companies led to lateral phases or even situations where the women quickly changed companies again, for example, because the new corporate culture was not a good match for their personal value system in the way they had hoped. Of the five subgroups, the flexible hoppers have been the group most affected by changes in labour market conditions for example during restructurings following the major Asian financial crisis. On the other hand, flexible hoppers benefited most from the opportunities opening up in Russia or from China's economic boom, since they were able to choose between a wide range of different job openings. This group of women take the potential risks of changing companies into account when planning their careers or can react rapidly to unanticipated situations by quickly changing companies again, if needed.

Mentoring and sponsoring has played a role to the flexible hoppers but they are not the most important career determinants; individual personality factors remain key. The women build strong external networks and also build strong alliances at their current employers.

Family has not been a key career determinant in this group. Most of the women in the group are married and have children. Based on their accounts, the women in this group have not experienced conflicts in combining their roles as career women and mothers. The women are primarily career-oriented, and have organized their lives to be almost completely liberated from domestic chores and duties by their spouses, families and housekeepers.

5. Lean on and move up

> A niche sub-type of women, those that `lean on and move up` have a strong focus on the career steps recommended by their mentors. They build their careers on the advice of their mentors and even follow them to different companies. Both parties - the mentor and the mentee - benefit from the alliance.

This group comprises only 4% of the total research group, a niche finding in the research. The sub-type applied to some Chinese women pursuing HR careers in mainland China and French women in the Communications field. None of the group have reached CEO or GM level, yet.

The factor of mentoring and sponsoring has been more important over the course of these women's careers than in the rest of the group. Relationships with one or more mentors have had a profound impact on the women's careers. The lean on and move up type is typified by a strong focus on the career steps recommended by their mentors. Their career position can be best described as external, guided and built based on the advice of their mentors.

Some women who had worked in five or six companies to date were categorised in this group. They have national mobility within their country but no overseas experience. The careers of the women in this group are boundaryless and can be described as linear with some unexpected twists. Since these twists have only been occasional and the women's careers have nonetheless been strategically planned, their career paths are categorised between ordered and emergent. The more reactive components typical of an emergent career path can be described by reference to the dominant determinant of this subgroup's careers: mentoring.

These women find their work fulfilling and their primary motivation is a desire to help others develop. This is combined with a desire to advance their own careers and be given greater responsibility along with wider decision-making authority. It is also noteworthy that these women are motivated to achieve as good a reputation in their field as possible, both within their companies and in their markets. One interviewee said, "I am the best HRD in China". Hence, subjective success criteria are particularly pronounced. The same instances can be found in the French cases.

One of the Chinese women followed her general manager to a new company on three occasions, while another changed companies at her GM's prompting on two occasions. Another woman mentioned reported two career changes in company that she undertook on the advice of mentors (a different one in each case). The women's relationships with the mentors, most of whom were general managers and female, were marked by strong mutual trust and exceptional loyalty on the part of the women. Both parties benefited from the relationships. The women benefited because they could be sure of support; the mentors gained from the women's local knowledge and from having an "extended reach" in their companies through the women. In one of the French cases, the mentor placed very high importance to his own image in the market shaped by the support of his female Communication Director.

These women's career paths could almost be termed "mentor-bounded", since they followed their mentors to new companies on multiple occasions. Their careers are bound to particular general managers rather than particular companies. The women explained that they have always regarded their success as closely linked to the strength of their relationships with these general managers. At various points in the interviews, the women noted that having a close, trusting relationship with one's general manager is extremely important for career progression. By working closely together with their general managers from an early stage in their careers, the women were able to become intimately acquainted with a variety of senior management styles. Their observations benefited their own career development.

The careers 'lean on and move up' women were closely linked to the reputation and success of their general managers. Two examples showed that this strategy also entails risks if the GM suffers a setback. One woman followed a female GM to a newly founded company that collapsed after a short time. These women's career direction is more linked to external loci, given their own career success is linked to a mentor from whom career opportunities emanate.

How can the career typology support coaching women leaders in their career building?

Career typologies with top women leaders are still rare in recent literature. The example of the five types which have been analysed here can offer guidance and inspiration for other women. The typology offers a tool for coaching women leaders. Mentor coaching is supporting women leaders in various ways, for example, by clarifying women's career orientation and defining career strategy. Upbringing, socialisation and environment influence women's own vision concerning their careers in management and their career targets. Women fulfill a variety of roles in their life, with many of them facing the so-called motherhood penalty. Others experience discrimination specifically against women in higher management roles. A coaching process which systemically builds in the main determinants for women careers in management can help to clarify women's questions with their career and supports the strategic planning of a management pathway. Typical questions and challenges which only arise for women leaders will also be encountered. Questions like inter-firm mobility, geographical mobility, expert career versus broader career as well as other important questions need to be topics of coaching specifically designed for women managers. Coaches can therefor use the international typology of women in senior management functions as frame for reflection.

Summary

> *Top women managers in the Global Women Career Lab built their careers mainly through local inter-firm mobility or global unbounded change of employers. These successful role models are strong in their career orientation and have taken internal self-responsible career positions. The family orientation of the majority is subordinate to the primary role of the executive.*

The benchmark for developing the typology for the Global Women Career Lab was the women's career paths. In addition, determinants that have a particularly high impact on the career paths were selected from the full list covered by the FemCareer Model (Al-Sadik-Lowinski, 2017). This enabled a very precise description of the different career types. The women's personalities and motivators were criteria that could be derived from the individual determinants.

There is not just one way for women to reach senior management, as has been clear from the ongoing international research involving top women managers in various countries. Of the five career types, three have been dominant in this sample. The Flexible hopper subtype stands out with forty four percent of the total research group, followed by the Unbounded global subtype and the Stop-and-Go women.

The Stop-and-Go subtype represents what other western researchers describe mostly in connection with women manager career paths. Societal influences, childcare organization constraints, the career of husbands and cultural norms typically affect women in the Stop-and-Go subtype most. It leads to career decisions and, as a result, career paths that consider the needs of others such as family member and spouses more strongly. In this global research involving a selected sample of very successful women in senior functions, this "typical female career type" ranks third out of five. It cannot be concluded from this research that women worldwide who reach senior management levels plan their careers mainly according to the needs of their families and relatives. The family orientation in most subtypes was classified as low to medium. Surprisingly, the results in this research do not show that women from Germany or Japan, countries with a low participation of women in senior management, are more represented in the stop-and-go group. In fact, the analysis showed that no women from both countries were in this group.

One hypothesis from the findings could be that the more difficult a gender environment is for women leaders, the less likely they can reach top management positions following the Stop-and-Go pattern. Another hypothesis is that Chinese women in overseas who are married with

foreign husbands change their initial very strong career orientation and adapt to their cultural environment by switching to the Stop-and-Go pattern.

The women in the sub-types with the highest percentage, the Flexible hoppers and Unbounded global, show a low family orientation and set their focus on their executive roles after becoming mothers. These women have a very high achievement motivation and assertiveness. Company external networking is very strong, internal affiliation with key decision makers in their recent employers is high. Women in both groups have different mentors and sponsors which they have approached actively. The main difference between the two most frequent types lies in the mobility. The high percentage of Russian women in the Flexible hopper career pattern must take into account the background of the country's political and economic situation. The Flexible hoppers change companies even more often than the Unbounded global women but do not typically work outside their home countries. The Unbounded global women go where the opportunities are and have almost no geographical limitations.

Mentor coaching is critical to supporting women leaders in various ways. A coaching process which systemically builds in the main determinants for careers in management can help to clarify women's questions with their career and supports the strategic planning of a management pathway. Typical questions and challenges which only arise for women leaders will also be encountered. As women worldwide are still the minority in top management, the career paths and patterns of successful role models can, and will, offer guidance and inspiration for other women. The FemCareer-Typology involving top women managers across cultures is one of the tools used at the Global Women Career Lab Coaching for women leaders.

The author and researcher:

Dr. Bettina-Al-Sadik-Lowinski is a researcher, author and certified international executive coach (MCC). Following a long management career in multinational companies, she has worked as an international executive coach and expert on diversity in Germany, Japan, China and France. In 2014 she founded the Global Women Career Lab, a worldwide research and training initiative for women in leadership positions. She is author of "How Chinese Women rise", which was also published in China and awarded with the excellent topic price of the Silk Road project, and of "Women in Top Management", one of the largest global research with a selected sample of top women managers women from various nations. She is speaker at international conferences and her work is covered by the international economical and management press. Originally from Germany, Dr. Al-Sadik-Lowinski lives in Paris, France and in Cologne, Germany with her husband and children.

Testimonials from the Global Women Career Lab

"International, authentic reports from female top managers from different countries combined with a sound scientific analysis of the growth factors for women in management. Insights across countries. Highly recommended!"
Professor Dr. Jutta Rump, Managing Director, Institut of Employability (IBE), University of the Economy and Society Ludwigshafen, Germany

„Full of valuable insights. A must read to understand how women career paths work."
Britta Bomhard, Supervisory Board and Chief Marketing Officer, US

„Female executives have many strengths. Great learnings for women around the world. A treasure research!"
Shelley Shen, Senior Director Human Resources, Communications and Public Relations, Saint-Gobain Pipe, APAC, Head of PAM-LAN- Diversity Institute, China

"Women need other women as role models in management in order to plan their careers more strategically and understand that the sky is unlimited for them. In the book "Women in Top management" 110 role models from various countries share their experiences."
Mari Nogami, President Takeda Consumer Healthcare Japan, Inaugural Chair of Women in Business AmCham Japan

The Global Women Career Lab research initiative also offers mentor-coaching for women leaders and training for coaches and executives who are supporting and developing women leaders.
For more information please contact Dr. Bettina Al-Sadik-Lowinski: alsadik@bas-coaching.com.

2. Deutsche Kurzzusammenfassung

Typologie der Karrierewege von internationalen Topmanagerinnen
Orientierungsmuster für qualifizierte Frauen im Management

Untersuchungen von Thornton zeigen (2017, 2018,2019), dass die Anteile von Frauen an Seniormanagement Funktionen im Weltdurchschnitt im Jahr 2020 bei neunundzwanzig Prozent liegen und seit 2014 nur langsam steigen. Im Kontrast dazu belegen andere Untersuchungen, dass höhere Frauenanteile in den Exekutive Teams von Unternehmen zu besseren Ergebnissen führen. Verschiedenen wissenschaftliche Auswertungen zum Beispiel von McKinsey (2012) und dem Petersen Institut (2016) zeigen, dass Unternehmen bessere Ergebnisse erzielen und ihren Profit dann steigen, wenn in ihren Führungsteams Männer und Frauen gleichwertig vertreten sind.

Gerade weil Frauen weltweit im gehobenen Management weiterhin in der Minderheit sind, können die Karrierewege und Karrieremuster von erfolgreichen Frauen, die bereits die Spitzen von Unternehmen erreicht haben, andere Frauen inspirieren und sie darin unterstützen, ihre Karrieren strategischer zu planen. Karrieretypologien, die die Karrierewege und -muster von erfolgreichen Frauen im Management systematisieren, können Frauen als Orientierungsmodelle dienen, um eigene Karriere Entscheidungen und Planungen auf der Basis der Erkenntnisse von Rollenmodellen vorzunehmen oder diese als Reflexionsrahmen, zum Beispiel im Rahmen eines Exekutive Coachings zu nutzen.

Internationale Typologien, die auf selektierten Samples von Frauen in Top Führungsfunktionen basieren, gibt es weltweit kaum. Wie in fast allen Bereichen der Managementforschung dominieren Studien, die mit Männern in Managementfunktionen gemacht wurden. In der Managementliteratur sind interkulturelle Typologien für Frauenkarrieren im Management auch deshalb weiterhin selten, weil die Komplexität der Datenerhebung in globalen Studien für Forscher hoch ist und der Zugang zu den richtigen Zielgruppen in bestimmten Märken eine Herausforderung darstellt.
Die Forschungen des Global Women Career Labs (Al-Sadik-Lowinski 2017, 2018, 2020) enthalten wertvolle Informationen über internationale Frauenkarrieren im Management und über weibliche Führungsstile in verschiedenen Ländern. Ein Ergebnis der globalen wissenschaftlichen Untersuchungen ist eine internationale Typologie der Karrieren von Frauen mit Top Führungsverantwortung. Die Typologie analysiert die Karrierewege und Muster, nach denen weibliche Rollenmodelle weltweit ihre Karrieren aufbauen und beschreibt die Merkmale und Charakteristika, die diese selektierten Frauen im Hinblick auf das Management aufweisen.

An der wissenschaftlichen qualitativen Untersuchung nahmen 110 Topmanagerinnen aus fünf Nationen- Russland, China, Frankreich, Japan und Deutschland- teil, die nach einem theoretischen Sampling rekrutiert wurden. Die Karrierewege dieses Pools erfolgreicher Managerinnen umfassen 500 Unternehmen weltweit und mehr als 21 Länder. Ein Teil des Forschungsprojektes wurde als Promotion von den Wissenschaftlern der Universität der Bourgogne in Frankreich begleitet. Die Erkenntnisse der globalen Untersuchung sind zwar aufgrund der bewusst gewählten qualitativen, auf Tiefeninterviews basierenden Forschungsmethodik nicht statistisch repräsentativ, jedoch handelt es sich um einen der größten qualitativen Datenpools weltweit zu diesem Thema und teilstatistische Auswertungen wurden dort vorgenommen, wo es aufgrund der Datenlage möglich war. Verschiedene wichtige Einflussfaktoren auf Frauenkarrieren im Management wurden in die Analysen basierend auf dem FemCareer-Models (Al-Sadik-Lowinski, 2017), welches die Landkarte der Untersuchung zeichnet, einbezogen. Ergebnis der Auswertungen sind fünf Karrieretypen von Frauen in Top Führungsfunktionen aus verschiedenen Nationen.

Fünf Karrieremuster von Frauen im Senior Management: Bounded – Unbounded global – Stop and Go – Flexible hoppers – Lean on and move up

Erstes Kriterium für die Entwicklung der internationalen Typologie der Karrieren von Frauen waren die Karriereverläufe der Topmanagerinnen. Hier wurde zwischen traditionellen, unternehmensgebundenen Verläufen, d.h. Karrieren, die in einem einzigen Unternehmen stattfinden, und Wechselverläufen unterschieden. Dabei wurde zwischen lokalen und internationalen Verläufen unterschieden. Geplante und proaktive Verläufe unterscheiden sich von Verläufen, die eher auf reaktive Karriereentscheidungen hinweisen. Weiterhin wurde untersucht ob die Frauen selbstverantwortliche oder eher fremdbestimmte Karriereentscheidungen treffen. O`Neil (2004) bezeichnet ein eigenverantwortliches Management der eigenen Karriere als Merkmal eines „internen Career Locus". Ein „externer Locus" dagegen weist auf Faktoren wie Glück oder den Einfluss Dritter als Hauptmerkmale der Karrieremuster hin. Daneben wurden verschiedene Bestimmungsfaktoren aus dem FemCareer-Model für Frauenkarrieren herangezogen, wie zum Beispiel die Karriereorientierung der Frauen, managementrelevante Aspekte von Persönlichkeit, sowie der Einfluss von Familie, Mentoring, Sponsoring und Netzwerken. Eine detaillierte Beschreibung der Kriterien und der wissenschaftlichen Hintergründe ist der englischen Originalpublikation zu entnehmen. Die englische Originalpublikation enthält auch die detaillierte tabellarische Übersicht der Karrieretypen und der Einflussfaktoren und eine Übersicht der prozentualen Anteile der Typen in den Ländern (s. Grafik 1 und Tabelle1).

Frauen im Topmanagement fühlen sich selbstverantwortlich für ihren Karriereverlauf und managen diesen strategisch

Die Ergebnisse der Analyse weisen darauf hin, dass die Mehrheit der 110 Frauen aus aller Welt eine selbstverantwortliche Karriere leben und einen „internal career locus" aufweisen. Sie managen ihre Karriereverläufe eigenverantwortlich und proaktiv. Die aktive Suche von Chancen, das Schaffen von neuen Feldern und Karrieremöglichkeiten sind bei der Mehrheit der Frauen ausgeprägt. Für diese Frauen gehören Karriereplanung, die Möglichkeit sich selber darzustellen und die Suche von Verbündeten zusammen. Sie schaffen bewusst Situationen, in denen sie sich und ihre Leistungen darstellen können. Sie gewinnen das Vertrauen von wichtigen Entscheidungsträgern, bauen die Beziehungen ständig aus und involvieren diese aktiv in ihre Karrierepläne.
Nur wenige der 110 Frauen schildern auch eher reaktive Merkmale und überlassen zeitweise Ereignissen wie Zufall, Glück oder anderen externen Einflüssen das Zepter bei wichtigen Karriereentscheidungen. Selbst bei diesen wenigen Frauen sind eine sehr starke Karrieremotivation und ein starker Fokus auf Karriere zu beobachten.

Die fünf Karrieretypen, die Ergebnis der globalen Untersuchung sind, stehen exemplarisch für typische Karriereverläufe und -muster von sehr erfolgreichen Managerinnen aus verschiedenen Nationen und Umfeldern. Diese Karrieretypen können von anderen Frauen im Management, die weiter aufsteigen wollen, als exemplarischer Referenzrahmen für Gespräche mit ihren Coaches oder Mentoren genutzt werden. Sie bieten den Frauen die Chance für sich selber den bestmöglichen Weg zu definieren, entsprechend ihrer Lebensplanung und Ziele. Im Exekutive Coaching kann die Typologie von Coaches eingesetzt werden, um Reflektionen anzustoßen und das Treffen individuelle Entscheidungen zu unterstützen.

1. Bounded

Diese Gruppe umfasst Frauen mit traditionellen, hierarchischen Karriereverläufen, die an ein einziges Unternehmen gebunden sind. Nur 7% der Gesamtgruppe findet sich in dieser Gruppe wieder. Die Karrieren der Frauen lassen sich durch eine starke Bindung an ihr Unternehmen beschreiben und können sowohl lokal als auch international verlaufen. Frauen in dieser Gruppe zeichnen sich aus durch eine hohe Flexibilität bei gleichzeitiger Adaptationsfähigkeit an die Belange ihres Unternehmens. Im Global Women Career Lab stellt diese Gruppe eine Minderheit dar, die es aber in die höchsten Unternehmenslevel schafft. Frauen aus Deutschland, Frankreich und China fallen in diese Gruppe. Russinnen und erstaunlicherweise Japanerinnen, bei denen man lebenslange gebundene Karrierewege hätte vermuten können, sind in dieser Untersuchung nicht in dieser Gruppe anzutreffen.

2. Unbounded global

Die zweitgrößte Gruppe des Forschungspools (28%) sind Frauen, die ihre Karrieren auch im Ausland verfolgen und dabei sowohl Land wie auch Unternehmen mehrfach wechseln. Die Karrierewege sind gekennzeichnet durch einen flexiblen Wechsel von Unternehmen, gerade in den ersten zehn bis fünfzehn Jahren des Aufstieges. Flexibilität umfasst das Land, Unternehmen und auch die Nationalität des Headoffices der gewählten Firma. Frauen in dieser Gruppe sind sehr selbstbewusst und haben eine hohe Leistungsorientierung. Sie planen ihre Karrieren durchdacht strategisch und reflektieren ihre Karriereambitionen und -ziele sehr ausführlich. Dieser Karrieretypus ist in der Untersuchungsgruppe am stärksten bei den deutschen und japanischen Frauen vertreten und kommt am seltensten in Russland vor, was mit der Gesamtsituation des Landes zu tun hat.

3. Stop-and-Go

Die Stop-and-Go Frauen (17%) machen holistische Karriereentscheidungen, in die sie andere Aspekte wie Partnerschaft und Familie häufiger einbeziehen als die anderen Gruppen. Auch diese Frauen machen Auslandserfahrungen und wechseln ihre Unternehmen. Dieser Karrieretyp lehnt sich an die wenigen international publizierten wissenschaftlichen Untersuchungen zu weiblichen Karrieretypologien an, die das hier vorherrschende Muster als charakteristisch für Frauen beschreiben. Auch Frauen in dieser Gruppe treffen ihre Karriereentscheidungen aus einer starken intrinsischen Motivation heraus autonom und legen Wert auf lebenslange Weiterentwicklung. Jedoch akzeptieren sie Seitenschritte, laterale Phasen und Pausen mit Rücksicht zum Beispiel auf Familie und Partner. Frauen in dieser Gruppe haben im Durchschnitt zwei Kinder und über 50 % von ihnen haben karriereorientierte Ehemänner, die in den anderen Gruppen sehr selten vorkommen. Sie erhalten zwar emotionale Unterstützung durch die Partner, aber eher wenig praktischen Support. Alle haben jedoch Unterstützung durch Kindermädchen oder Haushaltshilfen. Die meisten der Frauen in dieser Gruppe wollen bestimmte Aspekte der Kindererziehung bewusst nicht delegieren.

Es ist erstaunlich, dass keine deutsche Frau und auch keine japanische Frau entsprechend der Kriterien in diese Gruppe typisiert wurde.

Aufgrund der noch geringen Beteiligung von Frauen im Seniormanagement und der hohen Teilzeitrate in Deutschland, hätte man vermuten können, dass hier viele deutsche Frauen zu finden sein würden. Das Gegenteil ist der Fall. Eine Hypothese hierzu ist, dass gerade in Deutschland Frauen, die ihrer familiärer Rolle zeitweise mehr Raum in ihrem Karriereplan einräumen, weiterhin in der Mehrheit keine Top Management Positionen erreichen können bzw. wenn sie es denn schaffen, absolute Ausnahmefälle darstellen. Diese Hypothese müsste durch weitere Untersuchungen überprüft werden.

4. Flexible Hoppers

Frauen, mit rein lokalen Karrieren, die häufig das Unternehmen wechseln, sind in dieser Gruppe kategorisiert. Mit 44 % ist dieses die größte Gruppe der internationalen Untersuchung. Gerade die Russinnen und Französinnen sind häufig in dieser Gruppe anzufinden, aber auch in allen anderen Ländern sind die Flexible Hoppers stark vertreten. Sie haben in vier bis neun unterschiedlichen Unternehmen gearbeitet und zeigen eine starke Mobilität zwischen verschiedenen Arbeitgebern, die sie entsprechend der Aufstiegsmöglichkeiten auswählen. Die Frauen fühlen sich nicht an einzelne Arbeitgeber gebunden. Sie suchen nach Herausforderungen, wollen in ihrer Karriere weiterkommen und orientieren sich dabei hierarchisch nach oben. Dementsprechend wechseln sie Arbeitgeber dann, wenn ihnen Aufstiegschancen woanders angeboten werden. Ihre Mobilität gilt innerhalb ihres Heimatlandes, innerhalb dessen viele von ihnen für einen neuen Job umziehen. Die Frauen sind sehr durchsetzungsstark und wissbegierig, suchen geradezu nach Herausforderungen und wollen so viel und so schnell wie möglich lernen. Obwohl sie nicht im Ausland arbeiten, weisen gerade die Chinesinnen eine hohe interkulturelle Kompetenz auf und wechseln zwischen multinationalen Unternehmen unterschiedlicher Herkunft. Die Flexible Hopper Frauen beschreiben auch die Risiken von Unternehmenswechseln und einige zeigen laterale Phasen in den Karriereverläufen auf, immer dann, wenn eine neue Unternehmenskultur ihnen nicht liegt und das zu einem weiteren Wechsel führt. Sie sind auch die Gruppe, die von Veränderungen der Wirtschaft am stärksten beeinträchtigt werden oder im positiven Sinne profitieren.

5. Lean on and move up

Die kleinste Grupper in dieser Typologie mit nur 4 % ist eine Nischengruppe dieser Untersuchung. Diese Frauen richten ihre Karrieren stark nach Mentoren und Sponsoren aus, von denen viele Frauen sind. Einige folgen ihren Mentoren*innen bei Unternehmenswechseln. Sie folgen bei Karriereentscheidungen dem Rat ihrer Mentoren*innen und richten sich nach ihnen aus. Ihre Karrieremotivation ist eher extrinsisch geprägt. Besonders interessant ist, dass diese Managerinnen wechselseitige Vorteilsbeziehungen mit ihren Mentoren*innen knüpfen, bei denen beide Seiten stark profitieren. Ein Beispiel dafür sind Chinesinnen, die ausländischen CEO den Marktzugang ermöglichen und ihrerseits darüber in ihren Karrieren aufsteigen. Die Karrieren der Frauen in dieser Nischengruppe sind teilweise eng mit dem Ruf und Erfolg ihrer Mentoren*innen verbunden. Es werden negative Aspekte des Scheiterns der CEO´s auf den eigenen Karriereweg beschrieben.

Ergebniszusammenfassung

> Die Topmanagerinnen des Global Women Career Labs bauen ihre Karrieren durch lokale Unternehmenswechsel oder den globalen Wechsel von Arbeitgebern auf. Diese erfolgreichen Rollenvorbilder besitzen eine starke Karriereorientierung und verfolgen unabhängige, eigenverantwortliche Karrieren. Die Mehrheit der Frauen ordnet ihre familiäre Rolle ihrer primären Rolle als Managerin unter.

Hauptkriterium dieser Karrieretypologie sind die Karrierepfade und Karrieremuster der Topmanagerinnen. Daneben wurden verschiedene Determinanten basierend auf dem FemCareer-Models ausgewählt, wie z.B. den Einfluss von Familie, Mentoring und Networking, wie auch die individuelle Motivation. Aus der Verbindung beider Kriterien konnten die fünf Typen präzise beschrieben werden.

Es gibt für Managerinnen weltweit nicht nur ein Karrieremuster oder den einen richtigen Karrierepfad. Von den fünf Karrieretypen, die hier beschrieben werden, dominieren drei. Die Flexible hopper stehen für 44 % der gesamten Gruppe, gefolgt von den Unbounded Global und Stop-and-go Frauen.
Deutsche Topmanagerinnen gehören mehrheitlich zu der Gruppe der Unbounded Global Frauen, die weltweite Karrieren verfolgen und mehrfach in das Ausland umziehen. Daneben sind über vierzig Prozent der deutschen Frauen Flexible Hoppers, die Karrieren gezielt durch Unternehmenswechsel aufbauen und dahin gehen, wo Chancen warten. Das impliziert auch, dass sie der gläsernen Decke und möglichen Diskriminierungen mit der Wahl von Unternehmen begegnen, die gleichwertige Chancen für Frauen und Männer bieten. Für Unternehmen in Deutschland bedeuten diese Erkenntnisse, dass sie in der Zukunft im Kampf um die besten Talente weitere Maßnahmen ergreifen müssen, um talentierte Frauen zu gewinnen und zu binden.
Über alle Länder betrachtet sind die Flexible Hoppers, die sich auf Karrieren im Heimatland fokuszieren, die größte Subgruppe der Typologie und prozentual sind die Russinnen und Französinnen hier am stärksten vertreten. Chinesinnen in Europa adaptieren sich ihren neuen Umfeldern stark und zeigen, anders als Chinesinnen in ihrer Heimat, zu fast fünfzig Prozent Stop-and-Go Verläufe, in denen Frauen familiäre Belange stärker als in den anderen Subgruppen berücksichtigen. Die Mehrheit der Topmanagerinnen aus den verschiedenen Ländern in der wissenschaftlichen globalen Untersuchung des Global Women Career Labs bauen ihre Karrieren durch Unternehmenswechsel auf und sind dabei lokal mobil oder aber wechseln mehrfach das Land. Sie haben eine starke Karriereorientierung und treffen intrinsisch motivierte, unabhängige Karriereentscheidungen. Die Familienorientierung wird der Karriererolle untergeordnet.

Die in anderen Studien häufig für Frauen beschriebene Einbeziehung von und Rücksichtnahme auf familiäre Belange in Karriereentscheidungen, die zu Pausen, lateralen Phasen oder Rückschritten führt, ist in dieser Untersuchung anzahlmäßig erst an dritter Stelle, bei den Stop-and-go Frauen, zu beobachten. Auch die Frauen der Stop-and-go Subgruppe dieser Studie verfolgen eine primär intrinsisch motivierte Karriere mit Aufstiegsziel. Keine Frau aus Deutschland wurde in die Stop-and-go Gruppe klassifiziert. Ein Ergebnis, was nicht zu erwarten war, da gerade in Deutschland immer noch viele Frauen Teilzeit wählen sobald sie

Mütter werden. Dieser Trend in einem sozio-kulturellen Umfeld und einer Gesellschaft, die stark auf Teilzeit Mütter baut, führt in Deutschland weiterhin dazu, dass Frauen bereit sind ihre Karriereziele anderen Zielen unterzuordnen. Eine Hypothese zu diesem Ergebnis ist, dass gerade Frauen in Umfeldern mit noch wenigen Frauen im Seniormanagement keine Stop-and-go Karrieren verfolgen können, wenn sie in das Top Management aufsteigen wollen oder sie, wenn sie es denn tun, absolute Ausnahmeerscheinungen sind.

Die vorliegende Typologie der internationalen Karriereverläufe und -muster kann in systemischen Coaching Prozessen eingesetzt werden, die speziell auf die Belange von Frauen ausgerichtet sind, die eine Managementkarriere planen oder verfolgen. Das Global Women Career Lab bietet Mentor-Coaching für Frauen und Coaches basierend auf den Ergebnissen der globalen Untersuchung an. Mehr Informationen hierzu über die Autorin: Dr. Bettina Al-Sadik-Lowinski: alsadik@bas-coaching.com.

3. Bibliography

Adler, N. J., Izarelis, D.N. 1988. Women in management worldwide. New York: M. E. Sharpe.

Al-Sadik-Lowinski, B., 2017, More than half the sky? Descriptions and determinants of the career development of female Chinese senior executives working for multinational companies in China, Cuvillier.

Al-Sadik-Lowinski, B., 2018, How Chinese women rise, Cuvillier.

Al-Sadik-Lowinski, 2020, Women in Top Management, De Gruyter

Ankersen, W., Berg, C., 2018, Schlusslicht Deutschland, Allbright Stiftung

Arthur, M. B., Hall, D. & Lawrence, B. S. 1996. Handbook of career theory. (5th ed.). Melbourne: Cambridge University Press.

Arthur, M. B., Rousseau, D. M. 1996 and 2001. The boundaryless career. New York: Oxford University Press.

Betz, N. E., & Fitzgerald, L. F. 1987. The career psychology of women. Academic Press.

Catalyst. 2016: The world databank 2016: Labor force participation rate, female, estimated China 2014, http://www.catalyst.org/knowledge/women-workforce-china (Retrieved February 20, 2020).

Davidson, ML., Burke RJ., 2016, Women in Management Worldwide, taylorfrancis.com

De Fillippi, R. J. & Arthur, M. B. 1994. The boundaryless career: A competency-based perspective. Journal of organizational behavior, 15(4), 307-324.

Devillard, S., Graven, W., Lawson, E., Paradise, R., & Sancier-Sultan, S. 2012, Women Matter 2012. Making the Break through. McKinsey & Company.

Fietze, S., Holst, E., & Tobsch, V. (2011). Germany's next top manager: Does personality explain the gender career gap? Management revue, 240–273.

Gersick, C. J. G. & Kram, K. E. 2002. High-achieving women at midlife: An exploratory study. Journal of Management Inquiry, 11: 104–127.

Hartmann M. (2002) Leistung oder Habitus?. In: Bittlingmayer U.H., Eickelpasch R., Kastner J., Rademacher C. (eds) Theorie als Kampf?. VS Verlag für Sozialwissenschaften, Wiesbaden

Huang, Q., & Sverke, M. 2007. Women's occupational career patterns over 27 years: relations to family of origin, life careers, and wellness. Journal of vocational behavior, 70(2), 369-397.

Kirchmeyer, C. 1998. Determinants of managerial career success: Evidence and explanation of male-female differences. Journal of Management, 24: 673–692.

Lepine, I. 1992. Making their way in the organization: women managers in Quebec. Women in Management Review, Vol. 7, No. 3.

McKinsey, 2012, Women matter, https://www.mckinsey.com/~/media/McKinsey/Business%20Functions/Organization/Our%20Insights/Women%20matter/Women_matter_mar2012_english%20(1).ashx, zuletzt abgerufen 27.5.2020

Noland, M., Moran, T. & Kotschwar, B. 2016. Is Gender Diversity Profitable? Evidence from a Global Survey, Petersen Institut for International Economy.

O'Neill, D. A., Hopkins, M. M. 2013. Patterns and paradoxes in women's careers, in W. Patton (Ed.), Conceptualising women's working lives: Moving the boundaries of discourse, pp. 63–79. Rotterdam et al.: Sense Publishers.

Powell, G. N. 2011. Women and men in management. (4th ed.). Los Angeles: Sage.

Richardson, M. S. 1974. The dimensions of career and work orientation in college women. Journal of Vocational Behavior, 5(1), 161-172.

Richardson, M. S. (1996). From career counseling to counseling/psychotherapy and work, jobs, and career.

Sonnenfeld, J., Kotter, S.L, 1982, The maturation of career theory. Human Relations, 35: 19-46

Thornton, G. 2014. Women in Business: From classroom to boardroom. Grant Thornton International Business Report.

Thornton, G. 2015, 2017, 2018. Women in Business. Grant Thornton International Business Report.

Vinkenburg, C. J., & Weber, T. 2012. Managerial career patterns: A review of the empirical evidence. Journal of Vocational Behavior, 80(3), 592-607.

Weber, M. (1972). Wirtschaft und Gesellschaft – Grundriss der verstehenden Soziologie. Tübingen: Mohr.

REAL LOVE

XOXO

CUTIE PIE

CUP CAKE

SWEET PEA

YOU AND ME

I LOVE YOU

HUG ME

ALL MINE

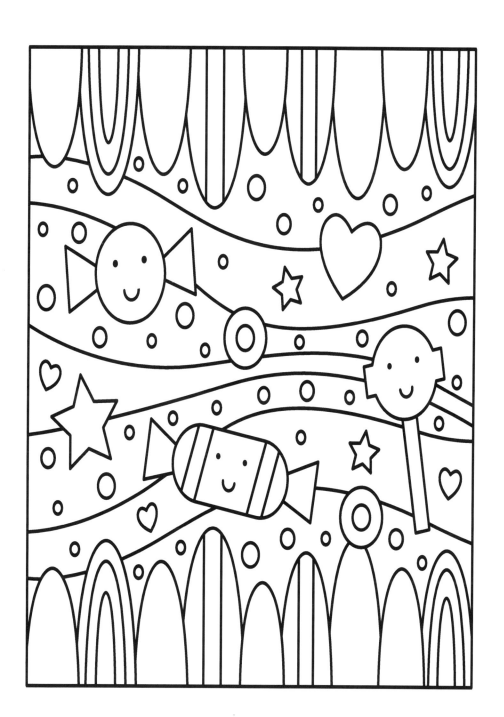

BE TRUE

SUN SHINE!

ONE I LOVE

TO MY AMAZING SON
HAPPY VALENTINE'S DAY!
COLORING CARD
Copyright 2018
by Florabella Publishing, LLC
All rights reserved. No part of this book may be reproduced in any form or by any electronic or mechanical means including information storage and retrieval systems, without permission in writing from the authors. The only exception is by a reviewer, who may quote short excerpts in a review.

YOU'RE SWEET

**Thank you for your recent purchase! We hope you've enjoyed your Valentine Coloring Card.
Happy Valentine's Day!
From florabella publishing**

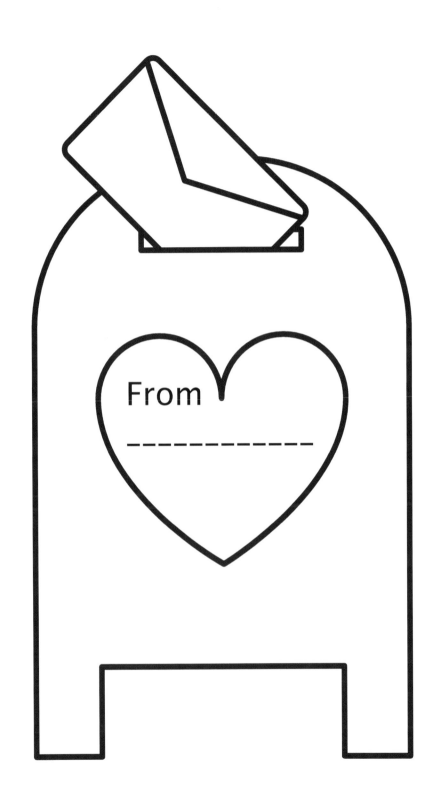

Printed in Great Britain
by Amazon